All Scripture references taken from the KJV of the Holy Bible, unless otherwise indicated.

The Swallowers: *Thieves of Darkness* by Dr. Marlene Miles

Freshwater Press 2024

freshwaterpress9@gmail.com

ISBN: 978-1-963164-33-6

Paperback Version

Copyright 2024, Dr. Marlene Miles

All rights reserved. No part of this book may be reproduced, distributed, or transmitted by any means or in any means including photocopying, recording or other electronic or mechanical methods without prior written permission of the publisher except in the case of brief publications or critical reviews.

Table of Contents

Swallowers 4
Power to Get Wealth 14
Without Offerings? 16
Signs of Idolatry 21
Powers that Swallow 23
The Elements 30
Where Are You From? 35
Serpents, *and Other Swallowers* 39
Earth, O Earth 42
You Can Swallow 49
The Armies 53
God Can 55
Too Big to Fail? 60
Three Days 63
Watch God 66
Put On Christ 75
Vomit It Up 76
You Are the Prophet 79
Warfare 84
Dear Reader 97
Other books by this author 98

The Swallowers

Thieves of Darkness 3

Swallowers

He hath swallowed down riches, and he shall vomit them up again: God shall cast them out of his belly.
(Job 20:15)

The enemy can steal the wealth of a man in many different ways--, too many ways, actually. One of the types of the thieves that come to steal from men was discussed in the first book in this series, **The Emptiers**. The second type and book is **The Wasters**. This book, number three, is about **The Swallowers**.

As we see in Jeremiah 51:34, there is an *emptier spirit*. It will allow you to stay alive, but you will be emptied of the good things in your life-- the important things. You may lose your money, and finances. They will make you a slave, working endlessly while seeming to achieve little to nothing.

The second type of thieves are the *wasters*. These powers wait for you to labor or gather to come and destroy what you've worked for (Judges 6:1-6). There are powers assigned to attack your marriage, business, ministry, or children after you have labored to have them and build them up.

This third type of thieves are the swallowers that we have been discussing. There is a 4th volume entitled, **The Devourers: *Thieves of Darkness: Why You Can't Have Nice Things.*** All of these *thieves of darkness* are ways the enemy employs to keep hitting your money and there is a reason for that. It's so you can't worship God properly, regularly and if you don't that makes you WEAK, and an easy target.

Sacrifice is part of your worship. He who worships God, God will glorify and empower for good works. If you are robbed financially, in the spirit, in the dream, and if nothing is done about the attack then it will manifest in the natural. If nothing is done about attempted spiritual robbery, the attacks will continue. Praying against the *thieves of darkness* can be prophetic and proactive--, or you can wait until something that you need, something that is yours is missing from your life, go into a panic and try to recover it. I wouldn't wait because the devil will try to make you into a cartoon character, looking around to see, *what happened?*

When the devil attacks, believe it – he is attacking more than the **obvious**. We are flesh creatures and what is natural seems to be the go-to when trying to figure out, what just happened. But the devil is strategic, so what is attacked or missing is really not that, or not that alone--, it could mean something else, and certainly *more* than that. As always with the spirit and spiritual things, add the dimension of **time** into an attack to help understand what the devil is after. Satan may not be after you at all, but your children, or your *children's* children. Or, he's after all of you, the entire bloodline.

Aside from taking away something that you need for life and godliness, or something that you enjoy, the devil wants to get you frazzled, and into a place of desperation. Do you know what desperation does to people? It makes them desperate and then they make stupid mistakes, such as turning to idolatry. The devil wants to create a problem or a need in your life and then step in like the super hero that he is **NOT** and fix the problem. In so doing he will sign you and your bloodline, your generations up by the evil covenant that was created.

The devil knows you can't serve God effectively with no money, no tithes, no offerings. How will you service your Godly altar?

What? An altar?

You have an altar, *right*? In the book, **Money on the Altar** we dealt extensively with altars, how they work, why you need one, and how to set up your own personal altar.

I thought the weapons of our warfare were this that and the other from Ephesians 6, you might say.

They are. Ephesians 6 describes personal armor; I'm talking about weapons of destruction. We cannot just lay those weapons down and retire them because they are in the Old Testament. The Old Testament people didn't have the Spirit of God **in** them, so they didn't have the particular weapons from Ephesians. But look at us, we can use the weapons of the OT **AND** those of the New Covenant and the New Testament. I'm not throwing out the Old Testament and neither should you.

The LORD has opened His armory,
And has brought out the weapons of His

indignation;
For this *is* the work of the Lord GOD of hosts in the land of the Chaldeans.
(Jeremiah 50:25-27)

Old Testament weapons abound in the Psalms. I don't see that book as just poetry; there is warfare in the Psalms. Some of those weapons are called and described in the Old Testament as the weapons of the time they were in. Weapons such as spears, the shields, the bows and the breastplates, (Nehemiah 4:16-18). Genesis 49:5 reads, *Their swords are implements of violence.* Whatever weapons you use for spiritual warfare be sure to use the Name of the Lord.

... a sword, a spear, and a javelin, but I come to you in the name of the Lord of hosts, the God of the armies of Israel,
(1 Samuel 17:45)

Do you think God put down His own spiritual weapons of the Old Testament when the New Testament came about? Lightning. Hailstones. Floods, Worship, The Finger of God. the Consuming Fire, the Rod of Moses, the Rod of God, the East Wind, the West Wind, the Great Wind, the Rumor of God, the Spear of God, the Flaming Sword of the Lord, the Razor of God. He can release locusts, worms, animals, and wasters. Yes, God created the wasters. And God has Mighty Warrior Angels, chariots of Fire, and others. Pestilence and all the plagues God unleashed on Pharoah. Hail, Blood, Boils, Death of firstborn, Frogs, Lice or gnats, Locusts, darkness, Flies, Killing the Livestock, drought, floods, cutting off their staff of bread, sending them into captivity. Bows, arrows and the modern, *and futuristic* equivalent of any and all of these weapons from Bible days.

All of these weapons of his armory are mentioned in the Old Testament. God can raise up and adversary against your enemies. He can send an army against your enemies.

And he answered, Fear not: for they that be with us are more than they that be with them. And Elisha prayed, and said, LORD, I pray thee, open his eyes, that he may see, (2 Kings 6:16-17).

Or, God can arise and do it Himself, contending with those that contend with you--, even the swallowers.

I can still use those Old Testament weapons or ask the Lord for use of the ministry of those weapons, and so can you.

God controls and uses the elements, and so should we. Sacrifices on an altar is in the Old Testament, but what do you think Jesus on the Cross was? Yes, the ultimate sacrifice. That sacrifice was for us, to redeem mankind back to God; for us to have Salvation. Thank You, Lord. And, even though Jesus has finished HIS work, we are still in the 6th day, the Day of Man and we are still doing our work, and walking out the plan of God in the natural. **We *don't* have *Nothing* to do.**

But isn't that such a human thing to do. When you get something new, you put the old thing out to pasture instead of adding to it, line upon line, precept upon precept.

You can and should enter into the Courts of the Lord **and** partake of the corporate altar in praise, worship and offerings. If you partake of that altar, then you contribute to that altar, right?

Else, *what are you doing?*

Anyone who is under spiritual attack needs to know that sacrifices make altars work. The more powerful the sacrifice the more powerful the altar, the more powerful will be the help you get from the Lord.

You are a dedicated saint of God, *right*? You are praying and praising and worshiping and studying your Bible? Fasting? Is your Godly altar alive? Is it burning? Are your offerings pleasing to God?

The Law of Approach describes what you need to do to approach anyone, and especially how you approach a King. You do not come before a king without a gift, an acceptable offering.

God is King of kings. As a king approaching another King, one who is higher than you are, what do you render? What do you bring. It is not about what's in your wallet, but what's on your altar? Does your offering, your sacrifice get God's attention and does God honor it?

Power to Get Wealth

The ability to deal successfully with money takes **power**, and that power is from God. Money is spiritual, so money management begins in the spirit. From God, we get the power to get wealth, and the power to **keep** wealth. We need the devourer rebuked, we need the *emptiers* scattered and the *wasters* removed from our lives, off of our money, and other valuable resources, in the Name of Jesus, Amen.

The *lust* for money is the root of all evil. Get rich schemes are famous swallowers of wealth. A person's hope investment could be swallowed up so quickly. When Bitcoin first became a thing, I was convinced to invest in it. Some weeks went by, and the value was rising, rising, rising. This was exhilarating. Wisdom is needed in any investment. Just as I watched the value rise at first, but then it began to go down day by day. Now, do we sit still and watch it go down and hope that it will rebound? Or do we withdraw it with profits. I'm one to withdraw it and take the profits rather than watch the stock market or bitcoin market swallow up my investments and increase.

Without Offerings?

No one can serve God effectively without offerings. Remember when the Hebrew slaves wanted to go to worship and Pharoah told them that they could go, but they couldn't take their livestock? Without the livestock there was nothing with which to worship God. Sacrifice is part of worship. If you have no money do not fail to go to church, but if you have an offering and do not give it, that is not pleasing to God.

Those who held back offerings, or any part of an offering, especially in a corporate service did not fare well in the Bible. Ananias and Sapphira. They didn't accidentally leave their checkbook at home when they went to church that day.

They had planned it and had agreed on what they would say regarding the tithe.

Therefore to him that knoweth to do good, and doeth *it* not, to him it is sin.
(James 4:17)

It is by Grace, and it is particular to each man, or to a family what the offering should be. Jesus sat by the offering basket; whether He did or not, how could the Son of God not know? How can God not know what you are placing on the altar? It is a test of faith, love, and honor to see what you will do with your own free will as it concerns the altar. It is a test of whether you will ignore the law and abuse Grace or not, to sneak past the altar without putting anything on it. And it is still a third test if you are asked about it, if you will lie or tell the truth.

But Jesus said, "Peter, let me tell you something. Before the rooster crows tomorrow morning, you will deny three times that you even know me."
(Luke 22:34)

That's three times you could by your own free will and not using Grace as an opportunity to sin, and also telling the truth that you can admit that you know Jesus, and that you are in the Kingdom of God. Instead, you are at church--, a *form* of godliness, but the real power is at the altar; if you don't partake of it you are denying the **POWER** of God. At the altar, where spiritual exchanges are made with the natural world, not the podium where the mouthpiece of God is standing.

Three times? Did I say three? It's four if you count the time that the Holy Spirit brings you under conviction for not hearing and obeying His instructions.

Three times. When something gets into a bloodline for three generations --, it's in there. Even though God sent 10 plagues and hardened Pharaoh's heart--, you're not a pharaoh, are you? Your heart should not be hardened to truth. Your heart should be pliable especially when it comes to the Word of God, the voice of God, and the Holy Spirit.

Three times, that same night, Peter said that he didn't know Jesus. How many times have you said that you don't know Jesus? In the sanctuary? At prayer time? At offering time? How many times have you said by your actions, or lack of action that you don't know? That you don't know His Word? That you don't know that He is a King? Or, that you don't know what to bring a King. Or, that you don't know how to bring a spiritually worthy sacrifice, Or, you don't know how altars work? How many times?

That would be like going to the market with no money--, how do you expect to get groceries? Admission to the movie cinema cost money—you didn't know? It's like that when you go to church without your wallet, checkbook, or phone app to put YOUR OFFERING on the altar. No one ever told you? You never read it in the Bible?

If your altar is cold, and the enemy's altar is not, which one do you think will win???

Signs of Idolatry

As said, what is on the surface may not be all there is to the devil's plan. If he is attacking your money, it's not just so you won't have money. We don't worship money--, we are not supposed to. We worship God, and money is a tool that represents our life, and blood, time, toil, and sweat that we place on our living altars to the ONLY LIVING GOD.

Check yourself, are you a servant to Mammon (money)? If you feel happy, et cetera when you have money, but depressed or sad when you don't, you might be serving Mammon. Most telling is if you are unable to put money on a Godly altar when needed, asked, told, urged by the Holy Spirit, or when you are about to go into warfare, or are in spiritual warfare, then Mammon may have a stronghold in your heart, and you need deliverance as well as doing the warfare against the thieves of darkness. Those thieves, recall are the *emptiers*, the *wasters*, the *swallowers*, and the *devourers*.

If you don't have, or service, or *priest* at an altar – no wonder the enemy is WHOOPING up on you.

Powers that Swallow

- Powers of my father's house that swallowed my testimony, that swallowed my breakthrough, that swallowed my prosperity, vomit it by Fire, by Fire, by Fire, in the Name of Jesus.

Serpents swallow. Serpents swallow breakthroughs.

An adult python can consume a deer weighing more than 70 pounds and alligators that weigh 100 pounds or more. Still, the little egg eater can consume prey with a cross-sectional area more than twice that of a Burmese python of similar weight.

The largest recorded animal eaten by a snake was a 150-pound hyena that was swallowed by an African rock python in

2017. National Geographic caught this on video, as a nearly 13-foot snake coiled around the hyena and began to swallow it. Snakes have stretchy skin and can swallow stuff four times the size of their heads.

The above describes swallowers in the natural. Spiritually, I'm sure we don't have to measure jaw arch size, head size, or mouth opening range---, but what **power** those demons are endowed with to swallow the blessings of God's people. That power is given to them by the hierarchal structure they are in and also, they gain power from humans who worship them. They gain power by blood sacrifices. There are sacrifices on evil altars, some of which may be working against you. those sacrifices are empowering things to swallow the good things in your life—your blessings. In the natural these things swallow:

- Reptiles.
- Crocodiles.

- Alligators.

There are representatives of these in the spiritual world, and also, there is *Leviathan*.

These swallowing beasts can ingest things of a far greater weight than what they weigh. When this happens in the spirit world, they swallow glory and destiny. There is a weight to glory and exceeding weight of glory. Some people may find these creatures cute or adorable, and want them for pets, but they are out to steal, kill, and destroy – don't get it twisted.

Evil human agents who practice the dark arts may have these animals, not just for pets, but they are considered family and roam about their houses. They employ them to "spiritually" swallow up blessings and even the lives of others.

Animals can swallow. Any animal can swallow--, a bird, a lion, any animal.

The following is in bold typeface for a reason: **If a swallower is sent to swallow anything of yours, it doesn't have to be bigger, or weigh more, it has to have more POWER than what it is trying to swallow.** The python coils around its prey and begins to swallow it. That lets us know that swallowing is different than gulping; swallowing takes a while. When things move slowly or take a long time, sometimes folks may not realize that anything is happening.

But the power it takes to make something stand still while it is being swallowed has to be pretty impressive. Saints of God, the prayers of the righteous makes POWER available to the person who prays. Saints of God, your weapons of warfare make you powerful. Saints of God, the enemy does all that to the negative, AND the dark agents rely heavily on their sacrifices on their evil altars.

Sacrifice is part of your WARFARE. Your sacrifice has to be greater than your enemy's sacrifice, unless your enemy, an evil human agent, a witch, or an occultist "loves" the devil more than you love God. How can they have more respect for the devil than you do for Jehovah, who is love and whom you say you love. Therefore, your sacrifice must be greater than the enemy's sacrifice, so you are not **overpowered.**

Saints of God: your pastor, prophet, church elder, deacon, or intercessor friend, can pray for you, or with you but they can't study the Bible <u>for</u> you. They cannot fast instead of you. They cannot praise or worship God *for* you. That's why the praise leader is screaming every Sunday, come on, Get Up, sing! Open your mouth and give God some praise!

Neither can they sacrifice for you. Job did for his kids, but you are no longer a kid, are you?

By the process of reading, studying, praising, praying, worshipping, the downloads and revelations that will come to you are specifically for you, for where you are in your spiritual seasons. No one can go get revelation that is intended for you, for you. Prophetic Words should be confirming what you know, or what you already suspect or what you've read in the Word.

This is one of the dangers of psychic prophecy from diviners and the like. That information comes from the second heaven, where the throne of Satan is. Psychic prophecy makes you dependent, since you're getting it from someone other than the Holy Spirit, then you stop hearing or listening to the Holy Spirit. So, now the information you are getting is either erroneous, wrong, or straight up lies, and you've turned off the Holy Spirit. This quenches the Spirit of God.

Yes, someone can give you a prophetic word, but every day, all day, when you, yourself need to be hearing from the Holy Spirit? You don't want your momma or your boss telling you all day what to do, then why would you want a lying stranger, or a lying demon to do it?

Hear GOD for yourself.

The Elements

Elements can swallow.

A tree a rock – they all have ears, and can be directed, programmed, instructed and enchanted to swallow. You've got to command any and all things that have swallowed anything of yours to vomit up your stuff, your blessings, your LIFE! Of course, proactively if you had commanded the morning, the night – the elements NOT to swallow anything that belongs to you, and not to obey the voice of evil enchanters, you might still be possessing your possessions.

The Earth can swallow. We read Scriptures to that end earlier in this volume. What do you think a sinkhole is? It is the Earth being swallowed, and it is formed to swallow anything in its vicinity. Many times, it does swallow. I've seen cars and houses in sinkholes.

- Any power that says I cannot have good things, nice cars or houses and they've come to swallow, let that power not touch my possessions, and DIE, DIE, DIE, in the Name of Jesus.

The sea can swallow. People can swallow. Death can swallow. Anything that is a pit, has a pit, a grave, an open sepulcher, a hole, a void, all those things can swallow.

- Every spiritual blackhole created to swallow anything of mine, anything about me, or any of my promises, blessings, glory, star, or destiny, implode and force my possessions out, and back to me, in the Name of Jesus.

Because the enemy wants to swallow up your things, progress, and life, **your job is to make yourself unswallowable** because all the good in your life that God has blessed you with and that you've also worked for is desirable to a demon. That demon can't get good things from God, so it steals good things from unsuspecting, weak, or *compromised* humans.

How can you be protected from these attacks? By becoming **unswallowable**. How do you do that?

- Be too big to swallow.
- Be too spiny, too sharp, like a porcupine. Put on the Word of God, the two-edged Sword.
- Be too bitter to swallow. Be toxic to your enemy so as not to be swallowed. **Be covered with, even soak in the Blood of Jesus.**
- Be more powerful than the enemy. The Greater One is in us, so the scales are tilted in our favor, as long as we spring into action. We cannot do nothing and expect something.
- Stay out of the enemy's camp.
- BE FIRE! Be too hot for the enemy. My life, receive Fire, become Fire, in the Name of Jesus!

- Be too heavy for the enemy. Let the weight of the glory you carry choke that demon, that serpent.

If you are being ripped off, *it is* because of evil covenants in place in your life and in your family bloodline by whatever witch or occultist–, however their imagination decided to curse you. Or, however they were taught to curse you–, it depends.

Since you were born, the devil has been studying you via *monitoring spirits* or *familiar spirits*, so when a witch or an occultist inquires as to how to curse or attack you, that witch or wizard is really asking what is the best thing to do the worst to you, and what is the best day to do it. So, the curse and the attack will be specific.

Is that not sobering to you? Yeah, the devil has a file on you, all for the purpose of stealing from you, killing if he gets a chance and destroying your blessings (unless he can use them), and the works of your hands.

- Walk upright before the Lord; be ye holy.
- Repent.
- Stay prayed up.

If a person is curse-able, it is because of sin and iniquity in their bloodline or in them personally.

Where Are You From?

Where you came from is very telling in knowing what is or could be in your foundation. Various types of witchcraft are practiced throughout the world. Where did you come from? Where did your people come from?

Many people leave home, or their homeland to find a better life, to leave that foolishness behind, but foolishness follows people. Witchcraft follows people, no matter how far away you go from your place of birth or origin.

It follows people by the markers in their blood. So, it may be where you are now that determines what style of witchcraft is coming at you, if you're under witchcraft attack, or where you come from--, or BOTH.

Notice all through the Bible people were named a name and then the place of their birth was indicated. I used to think it was that way because they didn't have passports, state or DMV identification cards, back then, and people named folks very common names, like Mary and John. But it is written in the Bible, as a physical and spiritual identification, and the place of your birth also written in their blood, it is written in your blood, in your DNA.

Jesus of where? Jesus of Nazareth. Even Jesus had markers based on where He was from. And the Bible says, *Can anything good come out of Nazareth.* That meant that the territorial *spirits* of Nazareth had instruction and probably satanic empowerment to HOLD people from Nazareth down. The devil has invested a lot of time to set up the evil spiritual infrastructure that is in place, in your place of birth, for example. As the devil wants worship, if you are locked into that location and he has figured you out, and how to get worship from you, whether you know it or not, why would he want you to LEAVE town or move away? If he can figure out how to hold you down, keep you down, keep you from either wanting to move or being able to move, then that fits the plan he has for your life.

That hasn't stopped happening, folks. Where you are from determines a lot in what and how you need to be praying now that you have put on Christ.

The point here is that if there are markers in your blood because of ancestral or other iniquity that draws the swallowers then you've got to fight. If the markers in your blood say, since you are from such and such a place, the people from that place can only go so far or rise so high in life. No matter where they are, where they go, how much education, demons know they have covenants in place to enforce that those people remain at mediocre levels, and the devil can send in the thieves of darkness, such as the *swallowers* to swallow up what they amass as they try to progress in life and break familial and generational barriers.

Serpents, *and Other* Swallowers

Swallowing *spirits* are on assignment against the saints of God. Those types are stealth. They lie in wait, and you may not even know that they are there. They are patient, but greedy, voracious.

Serpents swallow. Chief among swallowers in your life is a serpent, especially the household serpent because it's close and silent. It's waiting for the right moment to strike.

Reptiles, crocodiles, alligators, water spirits, great whales, and other beasts all swallow in the natural. Similar beasts are employed in the spirit to accomplish swallowing against people, especially God's people.

- *Snake spirit.* Feeding in the dream, that's from the *snake spirit.* The

spirit of the serpent is the one that caused the first sin in the Garden of Eden, and it is most predominant in the Earth. The goal is to defile you.
- Spirit spouse – most spirit spouses come via the evil marine kingdom; its job is to defile you, make you unattractive to God. It steals from you, blocks you from marriage to a real human, defiles and makes you unclean.

The unclean sat outside the gate of the city. How can you possibly be in the Courts of the Lord if you haven't even made it through the gates of the city, much less, the Gates of Thanksgiving?

> Then the LORD God said to the serpent, Because you have done this, you are cursed more than all animals, domestic and wild.
>
> You will crawl on your belly, groveling in the dust as long as you live.

And I will cause hostility between you and the woman, and between your offspring and her offspring. He will strike your head, and you will strike his heel.
(Genesis 3:15-16)

All of nature gets this, therefore, mankind, so should we. Animals know who their natural enemies are and how to avoid them or conquer them. Shouldn't we? God has given us authority over serpents, and dominion over animals so we can take authority, not so we can just know that we *have* it.

Command the serpent that has swallowed your blessings to vomit them up, in the Name of Jesus.

- Every good thing in my life swallowed by the household serpent, be converted to Fire and be vomited, now, in Jesus' Name.
- Live in holiness; don't play.

Earth, O Earth

I repeat, anything that is a pit, has a pit, a grave, an open sepulcher–, all those things can swallow. Many natural and formerly considered inanimate objects can swallow when instructed or enchanted to do so. The devil is wicked; his agents in the Earth are wicked; we must be wise and wiser.

The Earth can swallow. Here's the four-one-one on that, below, God is talking to Cain.

> Now you are cursed and banished from the ground, which has swallowed your brother's blood. (Genesis 4:11)

The Earth opened up and swallowed those who were rising up against Moses.

The earth opened its mouth and swallowed the men, along with their households and all their followers who were standing with them, and everything they owned.
(Numbers 16:32)

All the people around them fled when they heard their screams, "The earth will swallow us, too!" they cried.
(Numbers 16:34)

- Lord, as I walk in right standing with You, toward my destiny and fulfilling Purpose, let the ground open up and swallow all evil that is working against me, in the Name of Jesus.

Elements in and of the Earth can swallow. A tree can swallow and hide virtues. Rocks can, as well. You must command every element to vomit your virtues, your blessings, your joy, your health, your marriage, your wealth, your family, your children, your success, your ministry, your destiny, your legacy.

Strongmen guard the swallowed blessings. The kingdom of darkness is very structured. Like mission impossible, if you think you're going to bust into anywhere and take back anything that belongs to you without a plan, strategy, and POWER, you'd better think again. First of all, if you even believe your things can be swallowed, you don't even know where your things are, so how could you possibly go get them? You don't know if there is more than one strongman. You don't know the power and the authority that strongman is wielding. Will there be principalities or rulers involved? Worse, you may not know if you have any spiritual power yourself, or how to use it. Do you have enough spiritual power to overcome the strongman who is blocking you from the blessings that God gave when you prayed because God said *Yes*, and *Amen* to whatever you asked Him for?

The sea can swallow, the enemy's floods, and that flood swallows. Jonah went overboard in a sea storm. After that he was swallowed by a giant sea creature.

Don't let the floods overwhelm me, or the deep waters swallow me, or the pit of death devour me.
(Psalm 69:15)

This is what the Sovereign Lord says: I will make Tyre an uninhabited ruin, like many others. I will bury you beneath the terrible waves of enemy attack. Great seas will swallow you.
(Ezekiel 26:19)

Things in the sea that swallow, such as whales, great fishes, and Leviathan, the Lord Jesus rebuke you.

Now the Lord had arranged for a great fish to swallow Jonah. And Jonah was inside the fish for three days and three nights. (Jonah 1:17)

Death can swallow.

Let's swallow them alive, like the grave; let's swallow them whole, like those who go down to the pit of death.
(Proverbs 1:12)

This is a good time to note that the weapons the enemy of our souls uses against mankind were there from the beginning. Do you think the devil has dropped any of his evil weapons because that's what he used in the Old Testament, and we are in a different Dispensation right now?

Of course not; he may reinvent things; he may add to what has already worked.

I remind you again, altars work, sacrifices work, sacrifices on altars work. Sacrifices are required; God has required them from the beginning. We can't just drop financial sacrifices because we don't want to do them anymore. We can't just stop putting sacrifices on the Altar of God, declaring that they are Old Testament, because of the sacrifice of Jesus Christ.

By the which will we are sanctified through the offering of the body of Jesus Christ once for all. (Hebrews 10:10).

Yes, Jesus died once and for all. That does not mean that the Old Testament, and what is in it is no longer a part of the Bible.

There are some religions who only use a part of the Bible, mainly the Pentateuch and the Old Testament; they haven't gotten the revelation of Jesus Christ yet, or that He is Messiah. As Jesus said in the Gospels, O Jerusalem, Jerusalem, you missed your visitation.

Saying, If thou hadst known, even thou, at least in this thy day, the things which belong unto thy peace! but now they are hid from thine eyes.

And shall lay thee even with the ground, and thy children within thee; and they shall not leave in thee one stone upon another; because thou knewest not the time of thy visitation. (Luke 19:42, 44)

If man is so spiritually blind as to miss Jesus when He is walking among them for 30+ years, how should he trust himself to decide that part of the Bible is inconvenient, or he doesn't agree with it, so he will just skip past the parts that he doesn't like.

This is the kind of stuff that allows swallowers into a person's life, even into a Believer's life. Not putting a proper sacrifice on the Altar of God diminishes power for the Believer to fight any and all of the *thieves of darkness*.

You Can Swallow

You can swallow. That's not news, though, is it?

Worse, the enemy knows that you can swallow, that's what all that spiritual night feeding is about, to get you to swallow poisons and items that should never be ingested by a human. One of those things swallowed is the lie that the devil does not exist; he definitely does exist.

Sometimes the enemy is so crafty that he can get a person to swallow something of value that belongs to them – that is hide it from them inside of themselves… hey I don't make this stuff up – ask the Holy Spirit if this is true.

The devil can make you into a swallower and cause you to work against your own success. We have all probably heard of too many binge drinkers, who as soon as they get paid, or get any money, go to the bar and drink and drink and drink until the money is all gone. Their family does without because of the alcoholic swallowing up all his own increase. This swallowing applies also to drugs or other habits that use up resources for self-medication or entertainment. Addictions are bondages and deliverance is needed.

- Lord, in the Name of Jesus, I repent for things that I ignorantly swallowed myself. Take this evil yoke off of me, and set me free from this bondage, in the Name of Jesus.

Spiritual food, among other things is slow-release poison to activate sickness upon you at a later demonic, satanic, evil date.

- LORD let any chosen date on any satanic calendar, let no hour,

minute or second be appropriate to steal from me, or do harm to me, ever in the Name of Jesus. Time, work for me; work in my favor, and never against me, in the Name of Jesus.
- Lord, let every ticking on demonic time bombs, fail to go off against me, in the Name of Jesus.
- All spiritual food, evil plantations, demonic poisons, introject, or any other ungodly device gadget or substance **FAIL** and be spiritually removed or expelled from me, causing me no harm, in Jesus' Name.
- Father: detonate against the senders 7-fold, so that they know that Jesus is LORD, in the Name of Jesus.

To the positive there were at least two times in the Bible where God instructed a prophet and then an apostle to swallow a book or a scroll.

And he said to me, "Son of man, eat what is before you, eat this scroll; then go and speak to the house of Israel." So I opened my mouth, and he gave me the scroll to eat. (Ezekiel 3 :1 NIV)

And I went unto the angel, and said unto him, Give me the little book. And he said unto me, Take it, and eat it up; and it shall make thy belly bitter, but it shall be in thy mouth sweet as honey.

And I took the little book out of the angel's hand, and ate it up; and it was in my mouth sweet as honey: and as soon as I had eaten it, my belly was bitter. (Revelations 10:9-10)

God has a good purpose and a reason for whatever He instructs any of us to do. We obey God. What we eat or swallow under the anointing of God is to our benefit and to the praise of His Glory.

The Armies

People can swallow. They even swallow up other people. Especially the greedy are out to swallow others. But you are pure and cannot stand the sight of evil. Will you wink at their treachery? Should you be silent while the wicked swallow up people more righteous than they? (Habbabkuk 1:13).

Wealth is treacherous and the arrogant are never at rest. They open their mouths as wide as the grave, and like death, they are never satisfied. In their greed they have gathered up many nations and swallowed many peoples. (Habakkuk 2:5)

King Nebuchadnezzar of Babylon has eaten and crushed us and drained us of strength. He has swallowed us like a great monster and filled his belly with our riches. He has thrown us out of our own country. (Jeremiah 51:34)

The people of Israel have been swallowed up; they lie among the nations like an old discarded pot.
(Hosea 8:8)

God Can

God can swallow. And, the Lord can give you the ability, authority, and the power to swallow up your enemies, and be victorious.

They threw down their staffs, which also became serpents! But then Aaron's staff swallowed up their staffs.
(Exodus 7:12)

But the earth helped her by opening its mouth and swallowing the river that gushed out from the mouth of the dragon. (Revelation 12:16)

God can use the elements of the Earth to help us. *We* are supposed to speak to the elements of this world; they obey the voice of the Word of God when we speak it, in prayers, decrees and declarations. We don't just wait for witches and warlocks and wizards to take authority over the sun, moon, stars, Earth, rocks, sand, trees and waters to do harm to us before we do anything.

We should be exercising authority over all the elements of this universe to work for us and never against us. If you think about it, God put Adam and Eve in the Garden to dress the Garden. Whatever Adam named a thing, that was its name. You don't need to name a thing unless you are going to SPEAK to it, call it to you, or give it a directive.

Obviously, Adam and Eve weren't doing what they were supposed to be doing, so they both got fired from their Garden jobs. Jesus paid the price for us all and got all of us hired again – to dress the Garden. Now the Garden is wherever we are, in this whole Earth. **Speak.**

> Hast thou commanded the morning since thy days; And caused the dayspring to know his place; That it might take hold of the ends of the

earth, That the wicked might be shaken out of it? (Job 38:12-13)

That the wicked might be shaken out of it--, the wicked wouldn't need to be shaken out of it, unless they were **in** it. *Why are they in it?* Because that is what the wicked do. They are dedicated to their crafts and craftiness. They are anointed by darkness to do it, they are forced to do it, they are threatened to do it. They offer sacrifices to the devil and will stay up all night chanting evil into the elements while the Christians sleep.

Humans who party, or who used to party, going from the club to the bar have all kinds of energy. But when they get saved, suddenly they get tired. They are used to staying up until 2 or 3 in the morning, at least on weekends. Now that they are saved, they are the sleepiest bunch you've ever met.

Christians, to stay up handling spiritual business, ask for Holy Ghost anointing and pray, pray all night if that is what it takes, but at least command the sun, moon, stars and the elements that they will not smite you, they will not harm you, and that the proud waters will not swallow you! At least do that!

Holy Ghost anointing is far more powerful than demonic anointing --- so why aren't you inspired, motivated and up praying? Read this well, the devil anointed you to party, be up all night, sinning. You were on *remote* and didn't even know it. The devil had you to take your glory and your star to the club and use the goodness that God gave you to attract, Lord knows what that was out on the prowl to corrupt you.

God doesn't trick people. If you want God in your life and having authority over your energy levels, or alertness, for that matter, you will have to ask Him.

Before you were saved you were up all night *to get lucky;* it was bad luck, but you didn't know that at the time.

Evil human agents and evil powers have studied you and if you are an easy target, then they will readily come after you. If you are walking upright, prayerful, studious, worshipful and place regular offerings on the Altar of God you are NOT an easy target, and they will not attempt to attack you because they know they will be hit back, speedily and MIGHTILY.

- Evil powers with intention to swallow me or mine, I am not your candidate, we are not your candidates, in the Name of Jesus.

Too Big to Fail?

Swallowers swallow destinies, people, things, glory, wealth, health, marriages, business, careers, education, children, family, houses, fruit of your labor--, anything. They are Glory *swallowers*, and *wasters*, and *emptiers*.

- Glory swallowers, die, in the Name of Jesus.
- Foundational dragons that have swallowed my virtues, vomit them by force and by Fire, and die, in Jesus' Name.
- Every power that has swallowed my virtues shall vomit them now, in the Name of Jesus.

Your job is to make yourself **unswallowable**. Reviewing, Be too big to swallow. Be too painful, too sharp to swallow. Be too bitter to swallow. Be toxic to your enemy so as not to be swallowed. Stay out of the enemy's camp. BE FIRE!

Make the enemy afraid of you. How do you do that? By being a force to be reckoned with, by walking in your divine power, authority, position and by being **VIOLENT** in prayer.

You get BIG in the Spirit by the Word;– you grow up in and on the Word of God. What devil do you think wants a belly full of the WORD and the SPIRIT of God. Become unswallowable.

You get known and BIG in the Spirit by prayer – pray with the understanding, and in the Spirit, enlarge your tents, strengthen your stakes, become unswallowable.

Ask the Holy Spirit to build and keep a wall of Fire, a hedge of Fire, a mountain of Fire around you.

STAY PRAYED UP. Stay in the Spirit. Walk by the SPIRIT, stay out of the flesh.

Who doesn't like to eat or swallow *flesh*? (Vegetarians, you know what I mean.) Saints of God, when you're in the flesh that's the *flavor* the devil likes.

The enemy swallows things that GOD's hand is not on. The enemy cannot swallow GOD; so, have as much God in you by way of the Holy Spirit as possible. IF you are not in obedience to GOD then God's hand is not on you, or the things in your life.

Be too powerful to swallow. Too strong. Be too important to the plan of God to swallow. Be too steeped into your purpose and in God's timeline for your life to even be touched. God gives us power to keep wealth; He makes us too powerful to be ripped off by the enemies of God--, those *thieves of darkness.*

Three Days

Jonah got swallowed by a giant fish, a whale. He was in the belly of the whale for three days and then he was vomited up onto dry land.

Three days in the Bible is not just what we think is three days, Wednesday, Thursday, Friday. Three, biblically represents the Divine, wholeness, completeness, and perfection. Three is a good number–, Father, Son, Holy Spirit. Three in One is the Holy Trinity.

Three days in a whale or a tomb, not so good.

What did God do on the 3rd day? Dry land and plants were created on the third day. On the fourth day, God created the sun, the moon, and the stars. Water and sky animals were made on the fifth day, and on the sixth day, land animals and people were created. People were created to rule over everything God had created. Have you commanded the morning, saints of God? Have you spoken to the elements on a daily and regular basis?

Jonah was three days in darkness inside a sea beast – a whale? Inside a whale, shouldn't Jonah have been *dead*? Dead, but not yet digested. **Killed but not destroyed**.

They say something swallowed by a snake may take up to a month to be digested. Recently, scientists in the Florida Everglades cut open the stomach of an 18-foot Burmese python and dragged out a 5-foot alligator. The gator was intact, with only parts of its skin having been degraded.

- Pythons are notorious for swallowing gigantic prey—like deer, alligators and cattle—**whole**.

Just like Jesus said Jairus' daughter who all said was dead was only sleeping, the Word says that people are cast down but not destroyed. From that, I surmise the people and things may be swallowed down, but not destroyed.

We are troubled on every side, yet not distressed; we are perplexed, but not in despair; Persecuted, but not forsaken; cast down, but not destroyed; Always bearing about in the body the dying of the Lord Jesus, that the life also of Jesus might be made manifest in our body.
(2 Corinthians 4:9-11)

Jonah got vomited out on the third day and ultimately, on the third day God resurrected Jesus from the grave.

Watch God

Even if you, or something of yours is swallowed, watch God. It looked as though death had swallowed Jesus. He was in that tomb. He was cast down, but not destroyed. But three days later, God, the Father had resurrected Jesus. Death has lost its power to destroy because of Christ Jesus, Amen.

Swallowers swallow your *stuff*, virtues, blessings, gifts, talents, life – those are appetizers – the real intent is to **swallow a person**, their whole life and their destiny.

Jonah said within the whale that he was swallowed up, in the grave. He was in darkness.

Disobedient Jonah, complaining to the Lord about the plight that he caused for himself. *Really*? Lord, help us all because we do it too. It's so easy to see when it's somebody else. Lord, have Mercy on us.

From inside the fish Jonah prayed to the LORD his God. He said: "In my distress I called to the LORD, and he answered me. From the depths of the grave I called for help, and you listened to my cry.

You hurled me into the deep, into the very heart of the seas, and the currents swirled about me; all your waves and breakers swept over me. I said, 'I have been banished from your sight; yet I will look again towards your holy temple.'

The engulfing waters threatened me, the deep surrounded me; seaweed was wrapped around my head. To the roots of the mountains I sank down; the earth beneath barred me in for ever.

But you brought my life up from the pit, O LORD my God. When my life was ebbing away, I remembered you, LORD, and my prayer rose to you, to your holy temple.

Those who cling to worthless idols forfeit the grace that could be theirs. **But I, with a song of thanksgiving, will sacrifice to you.** What I have vowed I will make good. Salvation comes from the LORD."

And the LORD commanded the fish, and it vomited Jonah onto dry land. (Jonah 2:1-10 NIV)

And the Lord commanded the fish, and it vomited Jonah onto dry land. (Jonah 2:10)

And the Lord commanded the fish... and the Lord commanded...

Have we not authority over the fishes, even from Genesis? Why didn't Jonah command the fish, **himself**? Because Jonah was in sin and Jonah had lost his position of authority and dominion. Note also that Jonah called on the Lord, made a vow and promised to bring a sacrifice to the Lord. Of course, in a whale, Jonah didn't have his checkbook, so he made a promise to God.

Things getting swallowed up in your life, is because of sin – yours, or someone else in your bloodline. It is why this thing has come upon you. It is why you feel that you've been swallowed by the sea or hurled into it. There may seem like trouble all around. We may not know when it happened but thank God that you can discern that this is not the way life is supposed to be. Else, you'd accept it blindly and do nothing about it. But when you're swallowed up, defiled by sin, you are cast away from God's presence; you are outside the gate. God and His Presence are what you need to remedy this problem, so you should put down your sin, and idols and look toward God's Holy hill again. Seek the Lord. In your distress, seek the Lord.

Therefore, until repentance and right relationship with God begins or is restored, nobody in your bloodline, including you can speak the Word of God with authority and command the vomiting back up, or the return of your stuff.

Three days and three nights is any part of those days.

Those who live in certain cultures may better understand that any part of a day is considered the whole day. That is why when you give folks from another culture who now live in western culture, for example, an appointment, let's say at noon... it is Noon to that Westerner --- to people from other cultures that is appointment is that **day**, and that means any time in that *day*. (The shortest unit of observed time is a DAY in many cultures.) I've had to learn this. People from other cultures have had to learn how western culture works.

These folks with appointments aren't late according to their culture, as long as they get there some time in that day, they have kept their word.

For example, in the Bible, an Esther fast isn't necessarily a 3-day dry fast, but to westerners it is exactly that. Any part of a day is the whole day according to the Bible customs of the people of that day, and by extension, to any cultures except western cultures.

I've been trying to figure, for years, out how Good Friday to Resurrection Sunday morning was three days. Jesus was in the grave on Friday night, all day Saturday, and the early part of Sunday.

Okay, so how long was Jonah in the whale, swallowed up? How long was Jesus in Hell, in the Grave? Both Jonah and Jesus died, were buried (Jesus in a tomb, Jonah in a fish), swallowed and came back to life after three days and three nights. Jonah is a type and shadow of the death and resurrection of Jesus Christ, but Jesus was never disobedient like Jonah.

Jonah was swallowed but he wasn't destroyed. So, it seems as though, the swallower takes in what it is swallowing to hide it, isolate it, sequester it, lock it up.

Jesus was three days in the tomb, but He wasn't consumed or annihilated. Absent any manmade activities against a body, it takes more than 3 days for decomposition, or even for the bones to dry out. We know from Ezekiel that dry bones can again live.

I say all this so that we realize that nothing is too hard for God. And, if we are supposed to be able to do what Jesus did, and even greater things, then we should be able to call back swallowed things from where they are tucked away or hidden. We should be able to call back blessings, good things, careers, marriages, family, and children. We should be able, if we have repented and in right stead with God again, to call *ourselves* back out of swallowed situations. Speak the Word in authority to that demon, beast, or element that swallowed your stuff, or someone else's for that matter, and that thing must obey the thundering voice of the Word of God and vomit, vomit, vomit out all that it has stolen and swallowed.

We've seen it in the movies many times where someone is about to be caught with something illegal and they can't think of or find any place to hide it, so they swallow it. Criminals swallow diamonds that don't belong to them. People sometimes have incriminating notes, or things written on paper that they don't want anyone to see, and they will attempt to swallow that item. Some expect to see it again---, in three days after they've gotten away with the theft and the lie. Others who have swallowed pouches of drugs, for example, have died.

Three days out of the Presence of God is a very long time. The Word says that every morning there are new mercies, so that exile to outside of the gate is one day, as long as one can show himself clean again to the priest. But being swallowed is not the one day, it can be three days, like Jonah, like Jesus, like Lazarus, whom his friends and family said, *Lord, surely he stinketh by now.* Twice the grave tried to **swallow** Lazarus, but Jesus called Lazarus out of the grave, as well Jesus commanded the grave to release Lazarus.

Don't give up; nothing is too hard for God. Walking in the Love of God, have authority and Grace, we, like Jesus should be able to call people back from the depths of pits, traps, and defilements where the devil has ensnared them.

We don't always and forever do it for them, but sometimes people need help. Sometimes we need that one another ministry. Sometimes we need deliverance. Sometimes that person needing deliverance is *__us__*.

Put On Christ

Now, your things and stuff are not nearly as important as Jesus Christ, but you do need your things and stuff for life and for godliness. You need your things and stuff to worship and serve the LORD. Monetary instruments represent your life, your blood, sweat and tears to service your Godly altar.

Warning: half Christ and half world, is not putting on Christ. If you want answers to prayers you have to be all in Christ, shunning the world, else, your prayers are just going to make whatever *idols* you serve, knowingly or unknowingly, very angry.

Of a greater concern is that God is not pleased with mixed religions. I cannot over state that, saints of God.

Vomit It Up

That tells me that however long your stuff has been swallowed up, GOD can command it to be vomited back up again.

... he has swallowed down riches and he can vomit it back up again.
Job 20:15

The voice of the Word of GOD which doesn't return void has so much power and authority that even when you, little old you, speak it, it will perform. Be sure to speak it in faith.

I'm sure you've heard very anointed praise or worship songs. No matter WHO sings an anointed song, it is still anointed. A person who can't even sing can sing an anointed song, and if you are very critical you may say they chopped that song all up--, but that you have to admit that the Anointing was still on that song. God and the Heavens heard that song and it sounded amazing.

Michael W. Smith songs come to mind. One night I fell asleep with a ministry playing on my laptop. Into my sleep that video ended, and another began. The praise team of that second ministry started praising and worshipping and somehow it leaked into my sleep. *Waymaker* --, and I had to wake up and worship with them. That song was speaking to my spirit, even while I was asleep. The pure Word of God is stronger and more powerful than that. You speak it and all of the spirit world must stand at attention and obey. Everything except wicked man obeys the Word of God. Every element, the sun, the moon, the seas. The voice of God thunders!

And the LORD commanded the fish, and it vomited Jonah onto dry land.
(Jonah 2:1-10 NIV)

The anointing on the Word of God is mighty, it is so strong that even if you have a tiny little voice, it will Thunder in the spirit world when you speak it, and you are in right relationship with the Father.

If you pray the Word prophetically and stay prayed up, you will most definitely be unswallowable.

> Many are the afflictions of the righteous, but the Lord delivers him out of them all. (Psalm 34:19)

I'd say being swallowed by a whale is an **affliction,** *wouldn't you?*

> Do not rejoice over me, my enemy; When I fall I will arise; When I sit in darkness, the LORD will be a light to me. (Micah 7:8)

- Imagination of the wicked sponsoring the battles in my life, perish, in the Name of Jesus.

You Are the Prophet

The voice of the Word of God spoken by an intercessor, a prophet, a pastor, a prayer warrior--, even YOU. Anyone speaking the Word of God who is in their correct authority and position of dominion is masterful. Repent of the sin that got you in this sorry situation and get restored back into righteousness by salvation and the Blood of Jesus, so that you have the authority to speak the Word of God.

No matter how long it's been since it was swallowed, speak to what swallowed it and also to what was swallowed.

Even if it is YOU that has been swallowed – all wrapped up in sin, now that you're aware and have come back to yourself, speak. Pray and speak that Word of God with boldness.

Behold, the eye of the LORD is upon them that fear him, upon them that hope in his mercy. To deliver their soul from death, and to keep them alive in famine. (Psalms 33:19)

Deliver me, Lord from a famine of life, of light, a famine of GOD--, a famine of the Presence of God. God was not in the whale according to Jonah's speech. God did not go to hell with Jesus –, Jesus had to overcome all that by Himself. Jesus was in another town when Lazarus died. If God is with you, that makes you unswallowable. Jesus, who knew no sin, became sin for us, and gave up the Ghost. The only way that tomb was able to get Jesus was because of our sin, and that for the time when Jesus took on that sin, God had to turn His back on Jesus.

For us, Jesus took on sin and went outside the gate of the city, so we could go *in*.

If your virtues, blessings or life was swallowed you may be wondering, where is God; how could God let this happen to me? More than once in this book I've said that you must make yourself unswallowable. If by sin and disobedience evil comes upon you, God can't help you until you repent.

Even if your blessings, or promises were swallowed decades ago—that is not too long for God, as long as you are in Christ, or someone is interceding on your behalf, resurrection power can work in your life. As it comes to swallowing, regurgitating is still possible with God, by the Word of God.

But, beloved, do not forget this one thing, that with the Lord one day is as a thousand years, and a thousand years as one day. (2 Peter 3:8 NKJV)

So, it doesn't matter how long it's been since whomever or whatever swallowed up your virtues or blessings – **PRAY. PRAY** today.

When you've been in the whale long enough, or since you finally noticed that this or that is missing, do something about it--, pray.

Things that are swallowed by swallowers are swallowed whole and can be brought back up again--, pray.

I stress, you must make yourself unswallowable. The surest way to do that is to live a consecrated life.

Because it is written, Be ye holy; for I am holy. (1 Peter 1:16)

As long as you are HOLY: God's face is toward you. God's eyes are on you. God's Hand is on you; nothing can take you out of God's hand. God's favor is toward you. God's favor is life.

When the enemy wants to destroy a soul, first he **defiles** it, or tricks you into defiling yourself. God hates the impure and the defiled so He will be afar off from you. You will be afar off from God as well; you will be outside the gates of the city, when you are defiled. At that point the enemy will swallow or attempt to swallow you up --- with the final goal to be destruction.

Quickly, sincerely, and with a sorrowful heart, repent.

Warfare

I paralyze all powers swallowing my miracles, in the Name of Jesus.

Lord, swallow the pursuers of my destiny, and my life in Jesus' Name.

Let all my blessings that the enemy has swallowed, be vomited now, washed in Living Water, and returned to me, in the Name of Jesus.

I spit out every satanic food that has ever been put I my mouth, by myself or anyone, or any entity, in Jesus' Name.

I vomit all night caterer foods that I have swallowed, in the Name of Jesus.

Lord, if I have been duped into swallowing any blessing or anything of value that belongs to me and it is hidden inside of me, spiritually, help me vomit it out completely, and return and restore it to proper use, in the Name of Jesus.

I command all my blessings that have been swallowed to be vomited now, in the Name of Jesus.

Earth, O Earth, I command you to vomit my prosperity, health, marriage, finances, and ministry that you have swallowed, in the Name of Jesus Christ.

Every power swallowing my prayers or answers to prayers, die, in Jesus' Name.

Every satanic power that has swallowed my money, riches, wealth, or prosperity, vomit it now, in the Name of Jesus.

Let the Earth open up and swallow up all destiny killers working against me, in Jesus' Name.

Every evil bird or animal swallowing my successes or prosperity fall down and die, in the Name of Jesus.

O Lord, let every power behind the *spirit* of swallowing any good thing in my life, be paralyzed, in the Name of Jesus.

Every evil animal, beast, element, or anything swallowing the fruits of my labor be paralyzed and die, in Jesus' Name.

Lord, anything planning to swallow anything of mine let them get lockjaw, in the Name of Jesus.

I command them to vomit it up, retch and retch and retch and suffer and vomit, and then die, in the Name of Jesus.

Let the strongman assigned to watch over my swallowed blessings be unseated by Fire, in the Name of Jesus.

Let the satanic bank where my swallowed money, riches, or wealth is stored receive the Thunder of God and Hailstones of Fire, in the Name of Jesus.

I recover the money of my labour from powers that swallow money, in the Name of Jesus.

Every power of the devourer that has swallowed my finances, vomit them now, in the Name of Jesus.

Any of my blessings and testimonies swallowed by witches be converted to hot coals of Fire and be vomited, in the Name of Jesus.

Lord, swallow up death in victory, and wipe away all the tears from my face, in the Name of Jesus.

Every evil man or woman assigned as an open sepulcher to swallow me and my calling, receive speedy judgement or destruction, in the Name of Jesus.

Lord, enable Grace so that I may escape every pit and pitfall that has swallowed others before me, in the Name of Jesus.

Pit, O pit, dug for me, my family or anything I have stewardship over, hear the

Word of the Lord, you shall swallow the one that dug you, the ones that dug you and not me or mine, in Jesus' Name.

Grave, O grave, Jesus has defeated you and death, I reject untimely death and will not be swallowed by either of you, by the Power in the Blood of Jesus.

Lord, don't let the unrighteous, the ungodly swallow me up, or swallow my virtues or blessings, in Jesus' Name.

All blessings, virtues and destiny swallowed by the unrighteous and the ungodly, I command them in the Name of Jesus to vomit them back up and return them to me.

LORD, using the Word of GOD and walking in my divine position and authority command the fish to vomit me out onto dry land, in the Name of Jesus.

He brought me up also out of an horrible pit, out of the miry clay, and set my feet upon a rock, and established my goings. (Psalm 40:2)

Lord, bring me out of the horrible pit or any place where I have been swallowed or isolated, in the Name of Jesus.

Set my feet upon the rock, the Rock of Ages, in the Name of Jesus.

Lord, establish my goings so that I am in Purpose and never swallowable again, in the Name of Jesus.

I command the fish to vomit my virtues, my blessings, so they will be returned to me, in the Name of Jesus.

I command the serpent, the alligator, the crocodile, the animal, the beast, to vomit my blessings and my life, in Jesus' Name.

I command: Earth O Earth, hear the Word of the LORD and vomit out anything that is mine, intended for me, given to me, slated for me, or buried against me, in the Name of Jesus.

Every serpent up against me, swallowing my breakthroughs, livelihood, peace, anything promised to me by my Father –

hear the Word of the LORD, today you shall **vomit it up again,** in Jesus' Name.

Spiritual reptiles, crocodiles, alligators, anything that has swallowed, vomit up everything that is mine, in Jesus' Name.

Leviathan, the LORD JESUS rebuke you; vomit up everything of mine that has been stolen from me from my birth until now, in the Name of Jesus.

Lord, draw Leviathan out with a hook and his tongue with a cord, in the Name of Jesus. (Job 41)

Lord, in Your sore displeasure with Your great and strong sword punish Leviathan, the piercing serpent, the crooked serpent. Lord, slay the dragon that is in the sea, in the Name of Jesus.

Lord, break the heads of Leviathan in pieces, and give him to be meat to the people inhabiting the wilderness, in the Name of Jesus. (Psalm 74:14)

Lord, turn the tables, flip the script on my enemies, in the Name of Jesus.

Lord, stretch forth Your hand against evil animals that have swallowed up my wealth, blessings, virtues, glory, and destiny, and smite them and the powers empowering them, in the Name of Jesus.

Smite them with pestilence and cut them off from my life, cut them off from the Earth, in Jesus' Name. (Exodus 9:15)

Let the Earth open up and swallow my relentless pursuers, in the Name of Jesus.

Let hell open its mouth and swallow all my relentless pursuers, in the Name of Jesus.

I command any element that has swallowed anything that belongs to me to vomit it up, in the Name of Jesus.

Earth, O Earth, vomit up my blessings.

Sea O Sea, vomit out my blessings.

Any person, evil human agent that has swallowed my blessings, vomit out everything that is mine, in Jesus' Name.

Death, O Death Jesus has victory over you, vomit out anything that is mine, that should not be in your possession, in the Name of Jesus.

Lord, for my sake, swallow evil spirit nations (which are evil powers), let them be swallowed up and exist no more, in the Name of Jesus.

> Just as you swallowed up my people on my holy mountain, so you and the surrounding nations will swallow the punishment I pour out on you. Yes, all you nations will drink and stagger and disappear from history. (Obadiah 1:16)

Lord, let death stalk all my enemies; let the grave swallow them alive, in the Name of Jesus. (Psalm 55:15)

Lord, disappoint the devices of the crafty so that their hands cannot perform their enterprise against me, in the Name of Jesus. (Job 5:12)

Earthquake of God, let the ground open up to swallow every problem in my life now, in the Name of Jesus.

Lord, let the wickedness of the wicked swallow them up, in the Name of Jesus.

Lord God, everything of mine that was swallowed and is now vomited, let the resurrection power of Jesus Christ revive, restore, and bring life and destiny back to everything that was cast down, killed, or attempted to be killed BUT not destroyed, in the Name of Jesus.

God can restore money. God can restore health. God can heal wounds. And all those that try to swallow you shall be rebuked, in the Name of Jesus.

Glory swallowers on this street, die and release my glory, in the Name of Jesus.

Everything that I didn't even know was missing, everything I lost a long time ago, even as a child, even at birth or in the cradle, everything stolen from me that has been in the belly of a serpent, an alligator, a lion, any evil beast – even Leviathan… anything that has been lodged in the belly of the Earth, the sea or any other element – let it be vomited and returned to me after it has received the resurrection power of Jesus Christ to be alive and whole again, in the Name of Jesus.

Lord, cast down the imagination of the wicked against me, in the Name of Jesus. Strike down their strategies against me and quench the power they plan to use to exert their evil plans, in the Name of Jesus.

Arrows that fly by day, arrows of evil imagination for my sake, backfire, in the Name of Jesus.

Wicked imaginations to make me fail and suffer, backfire in the Name of Jesus.

LORD, help Thou my unbelief – anything that I didn't even know that I could get back again – my purity, my virtues, my glory, my destiny, my future, my family, my relationships, my kingdom marriage, my children, I claim it all and I command every swallower of any kind to retch and retch and be in misery and be in pain until they vomit up everything that is mine and return it to me, in the Name of Jesus.

Evil Swallowers, and the powers that sent you, run into the forest, run into the sea, bury yourself in the desert—wherever you come from – run away from me, be very afraid and run away from me, AND die, in the Name of Jesus.

Thank You, Lord.

I count it as done, in the Mighty Name of Jesus. Lord, You have put a new song in my mouth, even Praise unto our God.

Lord, let many see it and fear, and trust in the Lord. (Psalm 40:3)

I seal these declarations across every realm, age, era, dimension, and timeline from now to infinity, by the Blood of

Jesus, and the Holy Spirit of Promise, in the matchless Name of Jesus Christ.

Let every evil retaliation against this word or these prayers fail miserably and backfire to the senders, in the Name of Jesus. **AMEN**.

Dear Reader

May the Lord bless you richly and deliver you from every thief of darkness, especially the *swallower* who wants to swallow down your blessings, or even you!

The swallower shall vomit it up again, in the Name of Jesus.

May your life be full of all the good things the Lord prepared for you even before the foundation of the world.

Amen.

Dr. Marlene Miles

Other books by this author

AK: The Adventures of the Agape Kid
AMONG SOME THIEVES
Ancestral Powers
Barrenness, *Prayers Against*
Battlefield of Marriage, *The*
Beauty Curses, *Warfare Prayers Against*
Behave
Blindsided: *Has the Old Man Bewitched You?*
https://a.co/d/5O2fLLR
Churchzilla, The Wanna-Be, Supposed-to-be Bride of Christ

Collective Captivity, *Break Free From*

Courts of Marriage: Prayers for Marriage in the Courts of Heaven (prayerbook)

Courtroom Warfare @ Midnight (prayerbook)

Curses of Blind Men

Demonic Cobwebs (prayerbook)

Demonic Time Bombs

Demons Hate Questions

Devil Loves Trauma, *The*

Devil Weapons: Unforgiveness, Bitterness,...

The Devourers: *Thieves of Darkness* (Book 4)

Do Not Swear by the Moon

Don't Refuse Me, Lord (4 book series)

Dream Defilement

The Emptiers: *Thieves of Darkness* (Book 1)

Every Evil Bird

Evil Touch

Failed Assignment

Family Token (*forthcoming*)

Fantasy Spirit Spouse

FAT Demons (The): *Breaking Demonic Curses*

The Fold (5 book series)

    The Fold (Book 1)

    Name Your Seed (Book 2)

The Poor Attitudes of Money (3)

Do Not Orphan Your Seed (4)

For the Sake of the Gospel (5)

Fruit of the Womb:

Gates of Thanksgiving

Gathered

got HEALING? Verses for Life

got LOVE? Verses for Life

got HOPE? Verses for Life

got money?

How to Dental Assist

How to Dental Assit2: Be Productive, Not Wasteful

I Take It Back

Legacy

Let Me Have A Dollar's Worth

Level the Playing Field

Living for the NOW of God

Lose My Location https://a.co/d/crD6mV9

Man Safari, *The*

Marriage Ed. Rules of Engagement & Marriage

Made Perfect in Love

Money Hunters: Beware of Those

Motherboard (The) - soul prosperity series

Name Your Seed

Occupy: *Until I Return*

Plantation Souls

Players Gonna Play

Power Money: Nine Times the Tithe

The Power of Wealth *(forthcoming)*

Powers Above

Marriage Ed.: Rules of Engagement & Marriage

Mulberry Tree, *The* https://a.co/d/6JP7KqK

Seasons of Grief

Seasons of Waiting

Seasons of War

Second Marriage, Third--, Any Marriage

Sift You Like Wheat

Spirits of Death, Hell & the Grave, Pass Over Me and My House

Soul Prosperity soul prosperity series 3

https://a.co/d/5p8YvCN

Souls Captivity soul prosperity series 2

The Spirit of Poverty

StarStruck

SUNBLOCK

The Swallowers: Thieves of Darkness (Book 3)
https://a.co/d/4DxSZz6

Take It Back https://a.co/d/dZnVE25

This Is NOT That: How to Keep Demons from Coming at You

Throne of Grace: Courtroom Prayer

Time Is of the Essence

Too Many Wives: *Why You Have Lady Problems*

Tormenting Spirits   https://a.co/d/dAogEJf

Toxic Souls

Triangular Power *(series)*

    Powers Above

    SUNBLOCK

    Do Not Swear by the Moon

    STARSTRUCK

Uncontested Doom

Unguarded House, *The*

Unseen Life, *The* (forthcoming)

Upgrade: How to Get Out of Survival Mode

    Toxic Souls (Book 2 of series)

    Legacy (Book 3 of series)

Warfare Prayer Against Beauty Curses

Warfare Prayer Against Poverty

The Wasters: *Thieves of Darkness 2*

https://a.co/d/bs2UP7Y

What Have You to Declare? What Do You Have With You from Where You've Been?

When the Devourer is Rebuked

The Wilderness Romance https://a.co/d/jfkMlnj

- The Social Wilderness
- The Sexual Wilderness
- The Spiritual Wilderness

The Wilderness Romance series is not a romance novel series. These books are about relationships with people who are still in the **Wilderness,** how to avoid them, or what to do if you've married one.

Series:

The Fold (a series on Godly finances) https://a.co/d/4hz3unj

Soul Prosperity Series https://a.co/d/bz2M42q

Thieves of Darkness series

Triangular Powers https://a.co/d/aUCjAWC

Upgrade (series) *How to Get Out of Survival Mode* https://a.co/d/aTERhX0